J. Ferguson
1996

SIENA

GARDEN GUIDES

FUCHSIAS & BEDDING PLANTS

SIENA

GARDEN GUIDES

FUCHSIAS & BEDDING PLANTS

DAVID MYERS

Illustrations by
ELAINE FRANKS

A Siena book.
Siena is an imprint of Parragon Books.

This edition first published in 1996 by
Parragon Book Service Ltd
Unit 13–17, Avonbridge Trading Estate
Atlantic Road
Avonmouth
Bristol BS11 9QD

Produced by
Robert Ditchfield Ltd
Combe Court
Kerry's Gate
Hereford HR2 0AH

ISBN 0 75251 584 5

A copy of the British Library Cataloguing in Publication Data is
available from the Library.

Typeset by Action Typesetting Ltd, Gloucester
Colour origination by Mandarin Offset Ltd, Hong Kong
Printed and bound in Italy

ACKNOWLEDGEMENTS

Most of the photographs were taken at Bromesberrow Place Nurseries, Ledbury. The publishers would also like
to thank the many people and organizations who have allowed photographs to be taken for this book, including
the following:

Mr and Mrs Terence Aggett; Burford House, Tenbury Wells; Hatsford Fuchsias, Ledbury; Lance Hattatt, Arrow
Cottage, Weobley; Hereford City Parks Department; Hergest Croft Gardens; Mrs R. Humphries, Orchard
Bungalow, Bishops Frome; Mr and Mrs J. James; Mr E.A. Nelson; Mrs R. Paice, Bourton House; Powis Castle
(National Trust); Mrs Clive Richards, Lower Hope, Ullingswick; Royal Botanic Gardens, Kew; RHS Garden,
Wisley; Wakehurst Place (National Trust); Richard Walker; Mr and Mrs R. Williams; Wyevale Garden Centre,
Hereford.

Photographs of the following plants are reproduced by kind permission of Thompson & Morgan Ltd, Ipswich,
Suffolk: sweet pea 'Snoopea' and 'Cupid Mixed'; of primroses, by the author.

CONTENTS

Poisonous Plants

In recent years, concern has been voiced about poisonous plants or plants which can cause allergic reactions if touched. The fact is that many plants are poisonous, some in a particular part, others in all their parts. For the sake of safety, it is always, without exception, essential to assume that no part of a plant should be eaten unless it is known, without any doubt whatsoever, that the plant or its part is edible and that it cannot provoke an allergic reaction in the individual person who samples it. It must also be remembered that some plants can cause severe dermatitis, blistering or an allergic reaction if touched, in some individuals and not in others. It is the responsibility of the individual to take all the above into account.

How to Use This Book

Where appropriate, approximate measurements of a plant's height have been given, and also the spread where this is significant, in both metric and imperial measures. The height is the first measurement, as for example 1.2m × 60cm/4 × 2ft. However, both height and spread vary so greatly from garden to garden since they depend on soil, climate and position, that these measurements are offered as guides only. This is especially true of trees and shrubs where ultimate growth can be unpredictable.

The following symbols are also used throughout the book:

    ○ = thrives best or only in full sun
    ◑ = thrives best or only in part-shade
    ● = succeeds in full shade
    E = evergreen
    H = Frost hardy down to 5°C (23°F)

Where no sun symbol and no reference to sun or shade is made in the text, it can be assumed that the plant tolerates sun or light shade.

Plant Names

For ease of reference this book gives the botanical name under which a plant is most widely listed for the gardener. These names are sometimes changed and in such cases the new name has been included. Common names are given wherever they are in frequent use.

FUCHSIAS

FUCHSIAS HAVE BECOME IMMENSELY POPULAR in recent years. This is probably due to the wide colour range and exotic shapes of the flowers, together with their relative ease of cultivation. They also provide colour in the garden over a long period, from midsummer to late autumn. These qualities make them particularly valuable in the modern small garden.

Hardy varieties are especially useful for brightening rock gardens and shrub borders, after most of the other residents have ceased blooming. Half-hardy types are mainly planted in hanging baskets or containers and are grown outside from early summer until autumn, when they are returned to the greenhouse. Standard types are also bedded out after the risk of frost has diminished.

Varieties with small to medium sized blooms generally produce the best continuous displays and tolerate wet weather conditions better than large double-flowered types. These often prove to be shyer in flower production and may require the protection of the greenhouse to attain perfection.

PLANNING YOUR DISPLAY

The initial step is to co-ordinate the colour scheme of your display. Personal preference will determine whether you opt for strong

Fuchsia 'Thalia' in a sea of nasturtiums.

Plants in a wall-pot give the effect of a cascade.

colours or subtle pastel shades. The colour and texture of the backgrounds which are to support your arrangements need to be considered, to make sure that the flowers create a suitable contrast.

I always advocate experimenting with something new, as this provides a challenge, together with a sense of anticipation, in the garden. Fuchsias can produce stunning displays, both on their own, or when grown with other compatible plants. In either case suitable varieties need to be chosen to produce harmonious displays when in bloom. Growth habits and eventual heights must be taken into consideration.

Summer displays in conservatories can be enhanced by fuchsias in hanging baskets and pots. It is essential, however, that ventilation and shading are available to offset high temperatures in periods of strong sunlight.

Fuchsias prove unsatisfactory in the house unless positioned in a very light window. Insufficient natural light results in premature flower drop.

A gardener with imagination will find there are many ways to display fuchsias in the garden. Walls, pillars, posts and fences can be festooned with hanging baskets; patios, porches and drives bedecked with containers of all kinds.

PROPAGATION

Stock plants or 'Mother Plants' provide the shoots from which cuttings for propagation are taken. Cuttings can be taken during spring and summer, selecting non-flowering shoots with two pairs of leaves. Remove the

A fine standard fuchsia tones with impatiens at its feet.

A barrel of pendulous fuchsias and begonias gives a long display.

lower pair, apply rooting hormone to the base of the cutting and insert to a depth of 2cm/1in in seed compost with perlite or sand incorporated. The tray or pot is then watered and placed in a shaded situation, preferably in a propagator in the glasshouse or on the window-sill, where rooting should occur within fourteen days.

CARE AND CULTIVATION

Once they are well rooted, transfer the cuttings to 9cm/3½in pots. A proprietary peat potting compost, or soil-based John Innes no. 2, provide a suitable growing medium. Insert them to the same depth, lightly firm in and water. Now is the time they thrive on warmth, 15°C/60°F minimum if possible, until they become established. Watering is required whenever the compost becomes fairly dry. In order to produce a bush fuchsia, pinch out the growing tip above three pairs of leaves. If a standard is required leave it to grow on.

Eventually, when the plant becomes 'pot bound' and the roots emerge through the base of the pot, it will need transferring to a larger container. This could take the form of a hanging basket, or receptacle in the greenhouse or outside. The same compost may be used for replanting.

When positioning your fuchsias in the garden, it is most important to guard against the plants becoming 'cooked' during periods of hot sunny weather. 'Dappled shade' is what they crave outside, shaded greenhouses if they are grown inside.

During the summer, regular watering and liquid feeding is necessary, whenever the plants begin to show signs of wilting. Fertilizer containing nitrogen and potash in equal proportions is ideal.

PESTS AND DISEASES

Fuchsias, like many other plants, act as hosts to various insects and fungi.

APHIDS (Greenfly)

These make their presence known as white scaly skins situated on the upper surfaces of the leaves below the growing tip. They have been discarded by the aphids living on the underside of the leaves just above. Control with a proprietary aphid spray.

WHITEFLY

These reside on the underside of leaves especially just below the growing tip. The adults fly off when you shake the plant. The worst legacy of this pest is the black sooty mould, which grows on the sugary secretion exuded by the insects. This defaces the plant's appearance. Control with a proprietary spray.

VINE WEEVIL

The larvae of this elusive beetle are located in the soil. They are cream coloured, up to 1cm/½in long, with chestnut brown heads. They merrily chomp through the roots of your plants, causing them to wilt and eventually die. Dispose of grubs and affected soil.

Lilium 'Pink Perfection', fuchsia and nemesia.

Fuchsia 'Mrs Popple' is wonderfully floriferous and has the added merit of being frost-hardy.

BOTRYTIS (Grey mould)
Grey spores grow on dead or damaged plant tissue which can spread to healthy leaves and flowers. It is necessary to reduce humidity within the environment by adequate ventilation of the greenhouse and careful watering during wet weather.

FUCHSIA RUST
This shows as light green patches on the upper surfaces of leaves, which, when inspected from below, reveal rusty brown areas of spores. Reducing humidity deters this problem and also affected leaves can be removed and destroyed.

1. FUCHSIAS FOR HANGING BASKETS

*Fuchsias are the ideal plants for baskets,
which give their pendant blooms the best
possible display.*

PLANTING *a* BASKET

THE HABIT OF GROWTH of a large proportion of fuchsia varieties determines that their flowers are allowed to cascade downwards in mid-air. Hence the practice of growing them in pots and baskets suspended aloft, where the true beauty of the flowers can be appreciated.

1. Make up baskets in the greenhouse during early spring when plants are available.

2. Wire baskets require lining with moss or a proprietary liner in order to contain the compost.

3. 'Pinched', well-branched plants of pendulous or arching varieties, should be used. Five plants in a 35cm/14in diameter basket produce an excellent display.

Wire baskets, galvanized or plastic-coated, suspended by chains, are the traditional types of container. Plastic hanging pots, which do not require lining with moss, have become popular and are available in a range of styles and colours. Where space is restricted half-baskets of wire or plastic can be fixed flush against the wall.

4. Fill the basket with 'John Innes' or peat compost, to within 10cm/4in of the rim. Place the plants around the edge angling them outwards, with one in the centre if space allows. Firm around with compost, leaving an indentation for watering.

5. Hang in the greenhouse or place on a large pot and water thoroughly. They should be kept here until early summer, and watered whenever the compost becomes dry.

PLANTING *a* BASKET

SITING

It is important to guard against fuchsias becoming 'cooked' during hot weather. They crave dappled shade in which to thrive. A sunny aspect should therefore be avoided.

MAINTENANCE

Daily watering is normally required, except during wet weather when it should be withheld.

A balanced liquid feed of equal parts nitrogen and potash is essential for sustained flowering of your basket.

17

1. **'Cascade'** A free-branching pendulous variety with medium-sized flowers. Sepals are white, flushed rose-pink; the corolla is rose.

2. **'Harry Gray'** A double-flowered, compact, self-branching trailer. Sepals are white with pink veins; corolla white, pink at the base.

3. **'Autumnale'** A strong-growing trailer with red-bronze foliage. The single flowers have red sepals and rose red corolla.

4. **'Jack Shahan'** Single, large-flowered pendulous variety with pale pink sepals and a rose corolla. The growth is robust.

5. **'La Campanella'** Profuse semi-double flowers on a compact, freely branching trailer. Small flowers with white sepals (tinged pink) and a mauve corolla.

The **corolla** is the tube of petals around the centre of the fuchsia. The **sepals** are the outer 'skirt'.

5.

'Swingtime' A vigorous, large-flowered double with arching growth. Shiny deep pink sepals, white pink-veined corolla.

'Brutus' is a vigorous, floriferous, single hardy, with red sepals and deep purple corolla.

'Mrs Churchill' Semi-vigorous, single-flowered, lax-growing variety.

◆ *Difficult to grow because of its shy-branching habit.*

FUCHSIAS *for* HANGING BASKETS

'Marinka' A vigorous, floriferous, single-flowered variety, with a cascading habit of growth. Sepals shiny red with darker red corolla.

'Annabel' Strong-growing, double, upright loose bush. Medium-sized flowers, sepals white tinged pink, corolla white with pink veins.

'Coachman' Vigorous single, with an arching habit. Flowers medium-sized with salmon sepals and glowing orange corolla.

'Beacon Rosa' Extremely free-flowering, moderate-growing single, with upright habit, though arching when it flowers. Sepals bright pink with pink corolla.

◆ *This variety is often considered to be hardy.*

'Blue Satin' Large-flowered double, with white sepals and dark mauve corolla, white at base. Moderate arching growth.

'Leonora' Vigorous, free-flowering single. Medium-sized blooms have salmon-pink sepals and rose corolla. Growth upright and arching.

'Frosted Flame' Early-flowering single with pendulous growth. Sepals white, green tipped with pink inside, and long corolla.

◆ *Shy branching variety. Pinch out the side shoots several times.*

'Flying Cloud' Sturdy double, producing upright arching growth. Sepals white flushed pink, corolla white with pink veins at the base.

FUCHSIAS CAN ALSO BE USED TO GREAT EFFECT when incorporated with other types of plants, such as pelargoniums, petunias, lobelia etc., to produce a mixed hanging basket. The ultimate reward for all your efforts comes when you are able to relax on a warm summer's evening, watching the swinging blooms overhead.

'Red Spider' Prolific single with long crimson sepals and deep rose-pink veined corolla. Moderate growth, extremely pendulous.

◆ *Excellent variety for edges of containers and baskets.*

'Rose of Denmark' Semi-double with arching and pendulous habit. Medium-sized blooms.

'White Spider' Vigorous single with long pink sepals and white pink veined corolla. Growth loose, long and arching.

'Pink Galore' Attractive, shy-branching double, of medium vigour and pendulous habit.

◆ *Ideal to cascade down the front of a pot or basket.*

'Miss California' Early-flowering semi-double with long pale pink sepals and white pink-veined corolla. Thin-stemmed upright, arching habit.

'Pink Galore' provides colour around the base of this basket by cascading below the other flowers.

◆ *The grey helichrysum presents an ideal contrasting background.*

'Display' Extremely free-flowering, single, hardy variety with bushy habit. It has pink sepals and a deep rose corolla.

'Border Queen' Free-branching single. Sepals are pale pink, tipped green, the corolla violet, veined pink.

WATERING FUCHSIAS IN A HANGING BASKET every day can be demanding on the gardener, especially if he has several to maintain. If they are on a house wall, they can sometimes be soaked from within by leaning out of a window. Otherwise, install a permanent micro-irrigation system which will water the basket at the turn of a tap.

FUCHSIAS *for* HANGING BASKETS

Three separate varieties of fuchsia are planted in this 20cm/8in hanging pot. They are the double white-flowered **'Annabel'**, single pink-flowered **'Leonora'** and single mauve and white **'Border Queen'**.

◆ *Each of these varieties produces upright and arching growth, making them a compatible combination.*

2. FUCHSIAS FOR CONTAINERS

Fuchsias are extremely versatile plants for containers. Arching varieties decorate hard, unattractive edges, whilst upright and standard types provide the extra dimension of height.

UPRIGHT FUCHSIAS

IN LARGER CONTAINERS, a variety with an upright habit is required for the centre where it provides the necessary height. For this purpose, a half-standard fuchsia is excellent, as it produces a two-tiered effect. In full bloom it will give a dramatic extended display. Such plants are especially welcome beside a garden seat where one can admire the delicacy of the flowers.

1.

1. **'Joy Patmore'** Bushy upright growing single, having masses of medium-sized flowers. Sepals pure white recurving, corolla deep rose-pink.
2. **'Jack Acland'** Strong upright free-flowering single. Medium-sized flowers having pink sepals and dark rose corolla fading to reddish-rose.
3. **'Estelle Marie'** Strong free-branching upright single, with medium-sized flowers held erect. Sepals white with green tips. Corolla violet, white at base.
4. **'Celia Smedley'** Vigorous growing, shy-branching, large single flowered upright. Sepals white tinged rose, corolla vivid scarlet.
5. **'Cloverdale Pearl'** Self-branching bushy single, producing an abundance of medium-sized flowers. Sepals pink fading to white, corolla tubular and white.

2.

3.

4.

5.

Upright varieties are ideal
as a focal point in the
centre of containers to
provide height to the
arrangement.

Many upright growers
develop an arching habit
due to the weight of the
maturing blooms. This must
be considered when
positioning in the container.

UPRIGHT FUCHSIAS

Upright varieties should always be selected when planting in borders so that the flowers are clear of the soil.

'Thalia' (Triphylla type) Vigorous upright, late-flowering variety. Bright orange-scarlet blooms, freely produced.

'Rufus the Red' (H) Vigorous upright bush, producing medium-sized single flowers in profusion.

'Prodigy' (H) Strong-growing upright with medium-sized semi-double flowers. Bright red sepals, rich purple-pink corolla.

'Snowcap' (H) Upright bush with semi-double flowers. Sepals are bright red and shiny. White corolla, pink-veined at base.

'Dawn' Upright bush carrying masses of medium-sized single blooms. White-tipped green sepals, mauve-blue corolla, paler at base.

'Marin Glow' Upright, free-flowering single. Medium-sized blooms. Pure white sepals and deep purple tubular corollas.

'Lye's Unique' Very vigorous upright growth, freely producing medium-sized, slender tubular flowers.

'Lilian Lampard' Vigorous self-branching upright with medium-sized blooms freely produced. White sepals with pink-lilac, tubular corolla.

'Royal Velvet' Large double. An upright bushy grower with deep pink sepals and dark purple corolla streaked crimson.

'Swanley Gem' Upright single. Medium-sized flowers having recurved scarlet sepals with mauve scarlet-veined corolla.

'Morning Glow' Upright bush, producing medium-sized, semi-double blooms freely. Pale pink recurved sepals, lilac corolla.

UPRIGHT FUCHSIAS

When growing large-flowered types, an aspect sheltered from the wind is essential to avoid flower damage.

'Gypsy Queen' Upright, large double free-flowering bush, with swept-back red sepals and a mauve corolla.

'Mieke Meursing' (H) Compact, floriferous single. Upright with medium-sized blooms. Red sepals and pink veined corolla.

'Dollar Princess' (H) Bushy, upright double. The stems arch on flowering. Cerise sepals with rich purple corolla.

'Garden News' (H) Shy-branching upright with semi-double flowers. Sepals reluctant to recurve.

'Tennessee Waltz' (H) Upright and arching habit, with double flowers. Pink sepals and lavender rose-streaked corolla.

SPREADING FUCHSIAS

VARIETIES WITH AN ARCHING HABIT OF GROWTH are ideal for planting around the edges of the containers so that the flowers cascade down in front of them. In all cases, the containers have to be deep enough to allow the pendulous flowers of a mature plant to droop without trailing onto the ground.

'Quaser' Large double free-flowered trailing variety with white sepals and full pinkish-lilac corolla streaked white at base.

'Eva Boerg' Early-flowering semi-double with pale pink sepals and purple corolla, splashed pink at base.

'Gay Paree' Medium-sized double-flowering trailer. Reflexed pale pink sepals; the corolla is mottled with shades of pink and purple.

'Dark Eyes' Upright bushy grower producing medium-sized double blooms. Shiny deep red sepals, violet-blue corolla, rose at base.

'Annabel' Strong-growing medium-sized double with upright arching growth.

'Vanessa Jackson' Large single-flowered trailer. Flared salmon-orange sepals. Rose-red corolla streaked salmon-orange at base.

'Muriel' Profuse, large-flowering single with vigorous, cascading habit. Scarlet sepals, pale purple-veined rose corolla.

'Leverhulme' (Triphylla type) Vigorous upright free-flowering variety. Deep glowing-pink sepals and corolla.

'Enchanted' A prolific large double. Rose-red sepals with mauve corolla, streaked pink.

'Brutus' (H) Early-flowering single with deep pink sepals and dark purple corolla. Thin-stemmed, arching growth.

'Gartenmeister Bonstedt' (Triphylla type) Late variety with dark foliage, veined red-bronze. Bright orange sepals and corolla.

'Dancing Flame' Double with arching habit. Orange sepals, orange-carmine corolla, streaked lighter orange at base.

'Sunny Smiles' Large blooming single with arching growth which trails. Pale salmon-pink sepals, crimson corolla with paler base.

'Beacon' Strong-growing upright bush which arches in flower. Medium-sized single flowers with scarlet sepals and mauvish scarlet-veined corolla.

◆ *Use spreading fuchsias to trail around the edges of containers.*

31

CONTAINER DISPLAYS

POTS, TUBS AND TROUGHS are traditionally used as containers. However, old wheelbarrows, chimney pots, hollow logs or anything which holds sufficient compost to grow the plants, is suitable. Often these are placed on pedestals to enhance the display of the blooms, which only reveal their true beauty when viewed from below.

Fuchsias can be planted in association with a large variety of plants, to produce mixed displays.

Fuchsias can be grown in pots and subsequently placed close together to produce a solid bed of flowers.

'Thalia'

'Waveney Gem'

Nowadays, it has become customary to arrange these containers on patios amid the confusion of toys, furniture and barbeques, where children glean constant pleasure from 'popping' the bauble-shaped buds dripping in front of them.

CONTAINER DISPLAYS

Pelargoniums, lobelia, alyssum and busy lizzies were traditionally used with fuchsias, but recently people have become more adventurous with osteospermums, diascias, felicias etc.

In this arrangement of pots, the fuchsia flowers add extra variety and form to the coloured foliage of the coleus.

'Elfriede Ott'

'Olive Moon'

3. STANDARD FUCHSIAS

A very popular way of growing fuchsias is as standards. These forms can provide the gardener with really eye-catching displays.

TRAINING *a* STANDARD FUCHSIA

STANDARD FUCHSIAS or 'tree fuchsias' as they are often called, are grown so that the flowers are held high above the ground, where they are displayed to perfection. It is essential to choose varieties which are self-branching and produce flowers freely. They should also have an upright arching habit of growth to form a round head.

The rooted cutting is potted into a 10cm/4in pot during the spring and is left unstopped.

The plant is trained to a cane as it grows and flower buds are removed as they appear.

It is important that side shoots are present in the axils of at least four pairs of leaves before stopping.

The growing-tip is pinched out when the desired height is reached. This is usually at least 1m/3ft.

Once stopped, the side shoots quickly develop. The growing points should be pinched out after two pairs of leaves are present.

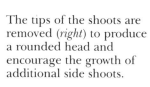

The head of a mature standard in spring (*left*) showing new shoots being produced on existing wooden branches.

The tips of the shoots are removed (*right*) to produce a rounded head and encourage the growth of additional side shoots.

Training a Standard Fuchsia

'Royal Velvet' creates a magnificent display of sumptuous, large blooms, shown to perfection.

This head is adequately clothed with sufficient shoots to generate a good, shapely display of flowers.

Repotting into a slightly larger pot should take place each time the compost becomes thoroughly filled with roots.

Water the plants whenever they become dry and begin to wilt.

Liquid-feeding, using a balanced fertilizer, enhances the performance of the plant once it begins to flower.

Check that the cane support is adequate and secure the plant to it as your standard develops.

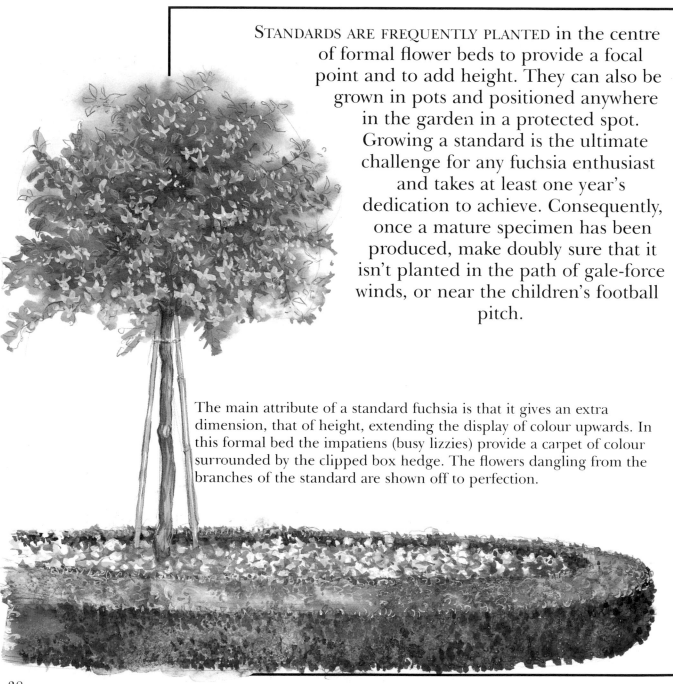

STANDARDS ARE FREQUENTLY PLANTED in the centre of formal flower beds to provide a focal point and to add height. They can also be grown in pots and positioned anywhere in the garden in a protected spot. Growing a standard is the ultimate challenge for any fuchsia enthusiast and takes at least one year's dedication to achieve. Consequently, once a mature specimen has been produced, make doubly sure that it isn't planted in the path of gale-force winds, or near the children's football pitch.

The main attribute of a standard fuchsia is that it gives an extra dimension, that of height, extending the display of colour upwards. In this formal bed the impatiens (busy lizzies) provide a carpet of colour surrounded by the clipped box hedge. The flowers dangling from the branches of the standard are shown off to perfection.

The bright pink-flowered standard adds height to the display of containers whilst extending the range of the pink colour scheme.

This standard serves to provide a pinnacle of colour and marks the position of steps to a higher garden.

An imposing display is created by positioning standards beside the entrance to one's house.

Plain areas of the garden can be instantly enlivened by the introduction of a standard grown in a pot.

A 'false' standard of a basket on a pole breaks up an expanse of patio.

Standards can be usefully placed to supply additional islands of colour and interest in established herbaceous borders.

A standard triphylla produces a focal point in a small bed and contrasts beautifully with yellow nasturtiums.

SITING *a* STANDARD FUCHSIA

A standard fuchsia has been aptly chosen to give height in a narrow bed beside a house wall.

◆ *It rises from a sea of harmoniously coloured nicotianas.*

'Border Queen' Strong free-branching single producing an abundance of medium-sized blooms.

The impressive effect of grouping standards whereby they form a wall round part of a garden.

◆ *Note that they have been arranged to take account of differing heights.*

'Devonshire Dumpling' Strong, compact, free-branching, arching growth bearing plump double flowers.

'Miss California' Early-flowering semi-double. Thin-stemmed, arching growth.

Both height and colour are brought to a border by a standard.

Tall fuchsias, arranged according to height, cascade forwards.

A fine combination for a large pot: *Fuchsia* **'Annabel'** above white marguerites, helichrysum and variegated foliage.

4. HARDY FUCHSIAS

A number of fuchsias are frost-hardy and can be planted permanently outside in the garden in those areas where the winter permits this.

A Star *of* Late Summer

FLOWERS OF HARDY FUCHSIAS are produced in the late summer until frost damages them in the autumn or early winter. In mild regions the top growth will survive on the shrub throughout the winter; whereas it will fail during a prolonged spell of low temperatures. In this case, the plants die down to ground level during winter. In spring, cut off the dead top growth. The fuchsias will produce new shoots from below the ground later in the spring.

'Eleanor Rawlins' A bushy, upright variety producing masses of medium-sized single blooms. The sepals are carmine with a magenta corolla, carmine at the base.

'Margaret' is a vigorous shrub. Here, beside a wall it reaches up to 1.5m/5ft within a single season. The colours of the flowers are enriched by bronze fennel.

Hardy fuchsias can be successfully planted to adorn paved areas where their blooms can be viewed from all angles.

Hardy fuchsias can be incorporated in herbaceous borders, as (in frosty areas) they die down to ground level during the winter and grow harmoniously beside their neighbours in the spring. In this group, the intense red and purple flowers of '**Mrs Popple**' co-ordinate well with the blue *Aconitum carmichaelii* and the leaves of the **purple sage**, and provide a rich deep background to the **lavender 'Hidcote'** in front.

HARDY FUCHSIAS

The golden foliage of *F. magellanica* **'Aurea'** provides a beautiful contrast to the green leaves and red-purple flowers of **'Bambini'**.

F. magellanica **'Aurea'** forms an impressive background to the dwarf-growing **'Tom Thumb'**.

F. magellanica gracilis **'Variegata'** Long arching stems are clothed with variegated cream, green and pink leaves.

◆ *The coloured foliage gives an additional attraction to this variety.*

F. magellanica **'Alba'** This variety sports bright green foliage bearing small single flowers with pale lilac sepals and deeper lilac corolla.

'Army Nurse' Vigorous, upright-growing variety. Small deep rose-pink sepals, purple corolla, veined with pink.

'Pee Wee Rose' This small single red-flowered fuchsia contrasts delightfully with the mass of finely cut silver leaves of artemisia.

'Dollar Princess' Sturdy, bushy, free-branching variety yielding quantities of medium-sized, double flowers. Cerise sepals with a purple corolla.

◆ *Tends to flower slightly later than most varieties.*

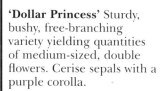
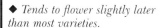

'Lena' produces an arching bush, bearing medium-sized double blooms. Pale pink sepals, deep pink corolla.

◆ Clematis *Jackmanii Superba' intertwined with the fuchsia adds interest to the plant.*

'Margaret Brown' Profuse-flowering, upright bush, sporting small single blooms. Rose-pink sepals, with a pale rose corolla.

'Checkerboard' Vigorous, upright-growing single with thin white curved sepals below a red tube and deep red corolla.

'Whiteknights Blush' The dark green leaves of this hardy fuchsia show off the delicate blush-pink blooms to perfection.

'Genii' Upright, bushy habit with yellow-green foliage and red stems. Small, single flowers of cerise and purple.

47

BEDDING PLANTS

BEDDING PLANTS ARE INVALUABLE IN THE GARDEN as they provide a continuous carpet of colour for a long period during spring and summer. They can be grown to great effect in borders next to the house, also beside lawns and paths. Island beds of various shapes and sizes can be introduced to enhance lawns, paved and gravelled areas. Essentially the beds should be formal in nature, providing a co-ordinated display.

During recent years many gardeners have resorted to planting perennials in their borders to reduce expense and labour. Shrubs and herbaceous plants, although a good compromise, don't provide such a lasting wealth of colour and adornment. They also command sizeable areas of ground when mature, which is acceptable in large gardens but unsatisfactory in small ones. Consequently, if you would like a dazzling display to beautify your house and garden, there is no substitute for the planting of annual bedding plants.

PLANNING YOUR BEDDING SCHEME

The range of plants and cultivars at your disposal is vast, especially in the case of summer

Narcissi and double daisies on a grand scale.

Cascading pelargoniums for baskets or window boxes.

Echium 'Blue Bedder' is a reliable hardy annual.

bedding. Many factors have to be considered when designing your proposed scheme.

1. Aspect, size and shape of borders.
2. Predominance of sunshine or shade.
3. Preferred colour pattern.
4. Relative heights of adjacent plants on maturity.
5. Planting distances. These will determine the number of plants required.
6. Cost of acquiring plants. This may influence the types chosen and the method of production.
7. Availability of the beds, if already occupied by your previous display.

This planning exercise is always pleasurable, especially if it is embarked upon during winter evenings by the fire. Seed catalogues, with their glossy images, are designed to seduce the enterprising gardener. They almost always succeed in persuading you to try new, ever more alluring varieties, which provide key points of interest in the forthcoming display.

ACQUIRING YOUR PLANTS

Once you have designed your bedding scheme, a decision has to be made as to how the plants are to be obtained. Traditionally, most bedding plants were raised by the gardener from seed in a greenhouse. This approach was the most rewarding, but required time and dedication.

Nowadays, several other options are available. Many seed firms and garden centres supply packs of seedlings ready for 'pricking out' (planting) into containers. Larger plants in the form of 'plugs' growing in individual cells, can also be grown on. Otherwise, garden centres and nurseries provide an extensive variety of mature plants ready for bedding-out into the border. This course is to be advocated where time and production facilities are absent.

GROWING FROM SEED

It is always exciting in the early spring to sow the first of your bedding plants in the greenhouse. The sowing times and cultural information about each variety are always documented on the seed packets. At this stage it is important to sow sufficient seed to produce the requisite number of plants for your scheme.

Many seeds, such as impatiens (busy lizzies), begonias, salvias etc., need warm seed compost in which to germinate. This can be provided by using a propagator which contains an electrically heated base, on which the pots or trays are placed. Alternatively, the germination process can be omitted by purchasing young plants of difficult subjects.

The sowing of small seeds is helped by mixing them with dry fine sand; this mix can then be sprinkled evenly over the level surface of the compost. Generally, seeds need only a light covering of fine sand or compost. Glass and newspaper are then placed over the container to keep the seeds warm and in the dark until the seedlings start to emerge.

Once the seedlings are large enough to handle and before they become spindly due to overcrowding, they are pricked out into bedding-plant compost in the greenhouse. Seed trays serve as the customary container

Tulips and double daisies give a dazzling display.

51

but an array of various sized 'cell trays' and pots are also available in which to grow plants with their own separate root systems. These remain in the greenhouse until they have utilized the space afforded them. They should then be large enough to transfer to the borders.

'Hardening off' the young plants acclimatizes them to outdoor conditions prior to planting. A cold frame is ideal for this purpose, as you can control temperature and watering according to the prevailing weather conditions. In the case of summer bedding plants, night frosts in spring present the greatest hazard and plants must be suitably protected.

PREPARATION OF THE BORDER

Prior to planting, the soil requires forking and breaking down to a fine tilth. A balanced fertilizer should be incorporated and the ground raked smooth. When planting large beds, it is advisable to mark them out with lines to determine the position of the plants. Sand or lime sprinkled over the prepared bed facilitates this. Several criteria affect the decision on when to plant your beds.

1. Resident plants of a previous bedding scheme may still be attractive.
2. The state of maturity of your young plants – are they strong enough?
3. Can night frosts be disregarded?
4. The border soil may be too wet or too dry.
5. You need to find the time and motivation to begin the job.

To maintain your border you must, first and foremost, guard against slug damage. In the country, however, rabbits or other pests may prove to be an even greater problem when they arrive for their breakfast. Watering is necessary during dry periods, especially until the plants become established. Weeds will also need to be removed.

Your bedding plants should now reward your efforts and produce an ever more spectacular riot of colour.

(*Above*) *Schizanthus* 'Hit Parade' or poor man's orchid.

(*Right*) Double daisies (*Bellis* 'Medici Rose') surround *Ornithogalum nutans*.

53

1. SPRING BEDDING

Bedding plants that flower in spring must be planted in the autumn, so need to withstand the frosts and wet of winter.

The myriads of flowers of the **myosotis** (forget-me-not) create an immaculate foil for the exquisite lily-flowered **tulip 'China Pink'**. The stems and leaves rise gracefully above the blue haze to parade the soft pink hues of the overlapping reflexed petals.

DURING PROLONGED COLD PERIODS, bedding plants become frozen and stop flowering. However, as spring approaches, they gradually come to life and reward us with ever increasing colourful displays of flowers. This transforms our garden into a cheerful and inviting oasis.

DISPLAYS *for* SPRING

Polyanthus require rich, moist, well drained soil in which to excel. Plant 30cm/1ft apart during early autumn.

◆ *The tulips follow an earlier display of daffodils.*

Universal pansies are planted 25cm/10in apart during autumn or spring.

◆ *Planting of summer bedding is often delayed as the pansies are in their prime.*

The contrasting drifts of **wallflowers, daisies** and **tulips** create a beautiful kaleidoscope of colour.

◆ *The terraces enhance the display by raising the plants.*

DISPLAYS *for* SPRING

FLOWERS ARE AT A PREMIUM during winter and early spring. Formerly, wallflowers and myosotis (forget-me-nots) were the traditional spring bedding plants, but the introduction of winter-flowering pansies has transformed the spring garden with an extensive colour range and long flowering-period. Ample reward is afforded for your efforts as you watch the first precocious blooms braving the elements.

Wallflowers and **Tulips** Single contrasting colours produce a more uniform display as all the plants grow and flower evenly, unlike mixed varieties. The tulips must always grow taller than their host plant so that their blooms are visible.

Wallflowers Well-branched plants should be planted 37cm/15in apart during early autumn. They thrive in well drained sunny borders and dislike waterlogged conditions. Fragrant. 30 × 30cm/1 × 1ft

'Ultima' and **'Universal' pansies** will flower during mild periods in winter and continue into the summer. 15 × 23cm/6 × 9in

The pansies provide a background of continuous colour, whilst the narcissi gradually emerge and dominate the display.

◆ *The pansies will reassert themselves once the narcissi have flowered.*

Daisies, polyanthus and wallflowers harmonize beautifully. The tulips provide the icing on the cake, decorating the wallflowers.

◆ *This demonstrates that mixed varieties can be integrated alongside self-coloured types.*

Myosotis (Forget-me-not) makes the ideal edging plant, or as a mass interplanted with tulips. 15 × 30cm/6in × 1ft

This is a colourful combination but the tulips can become lost amongst the polyanthus due to insufficient contrast.

Primroses grown in pots in the greenhouse and planted out in early spring produce a dazzling display. Fragrant. 10 × 15cm/4 × 6in

◆ *They are the 'Rolls Royce' of bedding. However, cost may prove prohibitive.*

DISPLAYS *for* SPRING

Bellis perennis **(Double daisies)** are available in shades of white, red and pink. They are ideal as an edging plant or for mass displays, interplanted with tulips. 15 × 23cm/6 × 9in

CULTURAL NOTES

It is important to bed out your scheme during early autumn so that the plants become established before winter. Growth ceases during frosty weather.

Once the bedding plants are in position, bulbs can be inserted in the gaps between them.

Little maintenance is required after planting, as normally sufficient rain falls from the heavens and weed growth is thankfully minimal.

SPRING BULBS

Hyacinths produce tubular spikes of florets which give off an exceptionally heavy fragrance, providing an extra aura in your garden.

Hyacinths can be planted out in the garden after being forced for use in the house.

Daffodils turn their flowers towards the sun. Remember to plant them in a position where they will face you too.

Except in a very formal scheme, avoid bedding out plants in rows. They will look more comfortable if intermingled.

Tulips like sun and a summer baking. In cold wet regions they are best lifted and stored in the dry before being replanted.

'L'Innocence' is an established hyacinth producing large sturdy spikes of beautiful white bells. 20cm/8in

Narcissus **'Sir Winston Churchill'** Vigorous, scented daffodil suitable for interplanting with wallflowers. 37cm/1ft 3in

Narcissus **'Roseworthy'** Delicate white petals of the perianth encircle the fluted salmon trumpet. 30cm/1ft

Narcissus **'Thalia'** produces up to three pure white blooms per stem. Ideal for the front edge of a border. 30cm/1ft

Narcissus **'Jenny'** Free-flowering, cyclamineus type. Suitable for fronts of borders and containers. 25cm/10in

Crocus Invaluable for providing colour in early spring. Broadcast bulbs in grass in the autumn and plant 5cm/2in deep.

◆ *Delay mowing in the spring until leaves have turned brown.*

Muscari (Grape hyacinth) Very easily grown in all types of soil and situations. Useful for edging and colour in difficult locations.

BULBS PROVIDE EXTRA COLOUR and add interest to your spring display. Many, moreover, unlike bedding plants, are perennial and invariably multiply over the years, giving excellent value for money. Many hybrid tulips are the exception to this rule but they are worth treating as bedding plants.

SPRING BULBS

Tulipa **'Noranda'** belongs to a late-flowering group of beautiful tulips whose petals have a crystal-like fringe. 45cm/1½ft

◆ *Pansies form the pale carpet beneath the tulips.*

Tulipa kaufmanniana **'Gaiety'** Commonly called the 'Waterlily Tulip'. This type is dwarf and very early flowering. 15cm/6in

◆ *The flowers require sunlight to open so plant in a south-facing situation.*

Allium aflatunense **'Purple Sensation'**, rises above pink forget-me-nots and white lychnis. 1m/3ft

◆ *This is a stunning, original mix of perennials and bedding for late spring.*

2. SUMMER BEDDING

Summer presents the gardener with a huge variety of plants for both formal and informal schemes.

PLANNING *the* SCHEME

YOU CAN PAINT A COLOURFUL DESIGN in your garden by using formal bedding schemes throughout the summer months. Conversely, informal displays, though often lacking visual impact, provide a continuity of interest as they evolve. The taller kinds of tobacco flower (nicotiana) are especially graceful in such arrangements.

Triphylla fuchsias create dark rich islands of colour amongst a drift of the marguerite, *Argyranthemum* **'Jamaica Primrose'**.

◆ *The contrasts of height and colour create an effective display.*

Impatiens, nicotiana and **ageratum** arranged in linear composition on a tiered border.

◆ *Respective heights of plants must be taken into consideration.*

A small-scale formal bedding display of mixed annuals in a domestic setting.

◆ *The grey-leaved cineraria makes a striking 'dot plant'.*

The realm of summer bedding embraces a wealth of plant forms, from the tall growing *Nicotiana* **'Sensation'** with its single star-shaped blooms and the large double flowers of **zinnia**, to the dwarf **alyssum** clothed with myriads of minute florets.

TALLER PLANTS

When planting remember to allocate adequate space as they may eventually grow over and smother their neighbours.

Additional support in the form of canes or sticks may be required.

TALL PLANTS located at the back or at the centre of borders provide variety and height. The selection here embraces annuals to be sown straight into the ground, half-hardy plants, bulbs, tubers and frost-tender shrubs which can be housed under glass in cold areas and planted out in the summer.

Asters flower later in the summer and are useful for providing colour when some bedding plants are waning. ○

Clarkia and the dwarf **candytuft** give a harmonious display when sown on site. Although not 'bedded out' these annuals achieve striking effects in a season. ○

◆ *These are good as 'fillers' and for creating colour in a dull spot.*

Argyranthemum **'Vancouver'** This free-flowering marguerite is a half-hardy perennial propagated from cuttings. ○

Cleome hassleriana **'Colour Fountain'** forms an idyllic background for the free-flowering *Penstemon* 'Garnet'. ○

Helianthus, the sunflower, is a favourite with children for its extra large blooms and height (2.2m/7ft). ○

Lilium 'Mont Blanc' can be utilized where height is required, without the plant spreading over its neighbour.

Abutilons Half-hardy shrubs which can be grown outside during summer and in a frost-free greenhouse in winter.

Helichrysum (Strawflower) provide a dazzling show of colour and are a favourite annual for dried flower arrangements. ○

Cosmos is a vigorous, bushy, upright annual and a most graceful addition to a scheme. Moist, well-drained soil. ○

Clockwise from top-left: a medium decorative dahlia; a cactus dahlia; a pompon dahlia; *Dahlia* 'Moonfire'.

◆ *Each of these types grows to about 1m/3ft and the tubers need to be planted at this distance. Half-hardy.* ○

PLANTS *of* MEDIUM HEIGHT

The hardy annual **Centaurea cyanus** (Cornflower) grows easily in any type of soil but requires plenty of light. ○

The flowers of **Salpiglossis 'Casino'**, a purple bicolour, can be used as cut flowers, although they are sticky to handle. ○

Dianthus barbatus (Sweet William) has a short flowering period and is usually grown as a hardy biennial. ○

The unusual colour of the mallow, **Malva sylvestris 'Primley Blue'**, is not readily found in other summer bedding subjects. ○

Zonal pelargoniums (Geraniums) are amongst the elite of bedding plants. They produce vivid displays during dry summers. ○

The dark red **nicotiana** form a good background for the pale pink **pelargoniums** edged with mauve **ageratum**.

◆ *This illustrates a perfect graduation of plants of differing heights.*

Heliotrope produces dark green, deep veined leaves which support corymbs of fragrant forget-me-not-like flowers. ○

Salmon **pelargoniums** are interspersed with mauve **verbena** and an edging is provided by alternating lemon-yellow **marigolds** with mauve **ageratum**.

◆ *This shows how to co-ordinate colours in an arrangement using different subjects.*

INFORMAL BEDDING SCHEMES are becoming more commonplace. Plants flowering throughout the summer can be incorporated into an existing bed or border to create extra colour. Many of the tender perennials, like the salvia below which can be grown early in the year from seed, are charming in informal schemes.

Nicotiana produce a profusion of blooms throughout the summer, and emit a sweet perfume during the evening.

Salvia patens produces vivid blue flowers and is useful as a 'filler' in informal bedding schemes of blue and yellow.

Salmon **nicotiana** overlook the brighter coral carpet of **impatiens**. Both of these plants produce spectacularly colourful displays over an exceptionally long period.

◆ *They thrive on warmth, therefore do not plant out too early.*

All of these plants illustrated require sunny aspects to perform well.

Plants which flower over the longest possible period should be chosen for formal bedding.

PLANTS *of* MEDIUM HEIGHT

White ***Osteospermum* 'Whirligig'** growing amongst blue nemophila requires a sunny situation for its flowers to open. ○

Sweet pea 'Snoopea' is unique in that it has no tendrils. The plant channels all its energy into producing flowers. ○

Tagetes produce masses of small orange flowers throughout the summer and the foliage emits a pungent smell if bruised. ○

Lantana are grown from seeds or cuttings and produce flowers throughout the summer months. ○

The uniformity of shape of these **African marigolds** is relieved by the mix of lemons and oranges. ○

A formal bed of mixed coloured **African marigolds** with an araucaria (monkey puzzle) as a centre piece. ○

Large flowering ***Tagetes erecta*** (African marigold) produces vigorous, erect, well-branched plants, requiring space. ○

Antirrhinums are among the first bedding plants able to be planted out and may survive another year in mild winters. ○

THE BRILLIANCE of many summer bedding plants can be utilized to produce large areas of colour in formal beds or to improve any dull or uninteresting part of the garden. Each year there is something new in the seed catalogues or garden centres to tantalize us. So be adventurous with your bedding scheme and you will always arouse interest and provide the element of surprise.

DWARF PLANTS

The mixed informal planting of summer bedding subjects succeeds in adorning a stone wall.

Purple **verbena** harmonizes with dark red **salvia**. The lemon **marigolds** and silver **cineraria** provide a lighter contrast. ❍

Tagetes patula (French marigold) are available in shades of yellow and bronze, as well as bicolours. ❍

During prolonged dry spells, watering is essential to maintain the production of flowers.

Marigolds are prone to damage by slugs when planted out. Protective measures must be taken.

71

DWARF PLANTS

Dwarf plants will provide a carpet of colour in which to position standard fuchsias as focal points.

The bright golden, daisy-shaped flowers of *Gazania* **'Dorothy'**, require a light sunny position to remain open.

*Felicia amelloides (***Blue marguerite***)* produces masses of small blue star-shaped Michaelmas daisy type blooms all summer. ○

The charming lilac *Nemesia fruticans* will flower all summer if dead-headed. Will tolerate light shade.

This carefully worked out bedding scheme has been arranged to flow gracefully around the existing evergreens: a conifer and hebe.

Chrysanthemum parthenium has pungently aromatic light green leaves with hosts of long-lasting flowers. ○

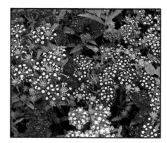

Verbena produce bright, rich coloured clusters of primrose-like fragrant flowers over a long period. ○

Salvia splendens is a classical formal bedding plant, producing a blaze of scarlet blooms on uniform compact plants. ○

◆ *Very tender plants which must not be planted out too early.*

72

Linaria maroccana **'Fairy Bouquet'** is available in distinct shades of pinks and mauves. ○

Schizanthus **'Hit Parade'**, the poor man's orchid, produces a wealth of blooms above deeply divided fern-like foliage. ○

Sweet pea 'Cupid Mixed' gives an abundance of scented flowers on a dwarf, bushy plant, which does not need staking. ○

DWARF PLANTS

Many of the plants illustrated here may be used as edging plants in the front of borders.

A dwarf **pelargonium** of the Angel group. Easily raised from cuttings, it has bushy growth and flowers that resemble violas. ○

Stocks can be grown in virtually any soil in a sunny position. They have a short flowering period but are very scented.

Begonia × *tuberhybrida* are among the elite of bedding plants and require fertile, sheltered conditions, with plenty of moisture, in order to excel.

◆ *The silver foliage of cineraria enhances the display with its contrasting colour.*

EDGING PLANTS

When planting beside a lawn, leave enough space to allow you to edge the grass as the plants mature.

***Senecio maritima* 'Silver Dust'** (cineraria) is used essentially for its attractive, white felted, fern-like foliage. ○

Begonia semperflorens are extremely free-flowering and are able to survive a hot sunny dry position.

Echeverias are advantageous for hot dry spots as their rosettes of leathery leaves resist drought. ○

Calendula (marigold) is one of the oldest of bedding plants. It thrives in the poorest of soils and readily self-seeds. ○

Impatiens (Busy Lizzie) are grown extensively as they can be relied on to produce carpets of colour in the garden, from planting until the autumn frosts.

◆ *They must be watered regularly during dry interludes if they are to thrive.*

Lobularia maritima *(Alyssum maritimum)* is a traditional edging plant and is available in shades of white, pink and lilac. ○

FORMAL FLOWER BEDS are traditionally edged with compact, dwarf plants. Single colours or varieties may be used, or several can be alternated, to create contrasting effects. A thin line of plants forming a ribbon will always look formal or artificial; flowing drifts of varying width will seem more relaxed especially if the plants are chosen to spill forward.

Petunia **'Ultra Star'** series give excellent displays during dry periods but flowers turn brown in prolonged wet weather. O

Colour co-ordinate your edge with the other plants in the border so that they produce a suitable contrast.

Diascias are some of the most prolific flowering plants. They thrive in a sunny situation but require watering to perform well.

Mesembryanthemum (Livingstone daisy) thrives in dry sunny sites as the brilliant flowers only open in bright sunshine.

Osteospermums continually produce white or mauve daisy-shaped blooms which close up towards evening.

Iberis (candytuft) is a free-flowering plant which will tolerate poor soil conditions and a dry situation. O

Ageratum produces compact mounds of flowers over a long period. O

◆ *Another good blue half-hardy annual is lobelia.*

Senecio maritimus (Cineraria) can be planted to form islands of silver foliage rising above carpets of **impatiens**.

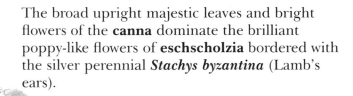

The broad upright majestic leaves and bright flowers of the **canna** dominate the brilliant poppy-like flowers of **eschscholzia** bordered with the silver perennial *Stachys byzantina* (Lamb's ears).

'DOT' PLANTS

The large palmate leaves of **Ricinus communis** (Castor oil plant) make an unusual and interesting focal point amid drifts of **impatiens**.

'DOT' PLANTS PROVIDE FOCAL POINTS of interest among areas of summer bedding. They can be short or tall, and they can form an isolated incident, or be inserted to form a repeat planting at intervals, but in either case it is essential that they must distinguish themselves from their surrounding bedding. Usually large pot-grown subjects are bought or raised at home under glass for this purpose, and then put in the ground at a suitable time for planting.

Angel's Trumpet
(Brugmansia, syn. datura)
Impressive focal point if grown as a standard. ○

◆ *Grow amongst heliotrope for a wonderfully scented combination.*